He asked his friends to come and see,

If they could eat from a to z.

almost lost
in applesauce

buried his head
in banana bread

collided with a carrot cake

devoured
donuts

ecstatic
over
eclairs

fast asleep and
full of figs

gobbled
grapes

hollered "hooray" for honey

indulged in ice cream

jiggled Jell-O

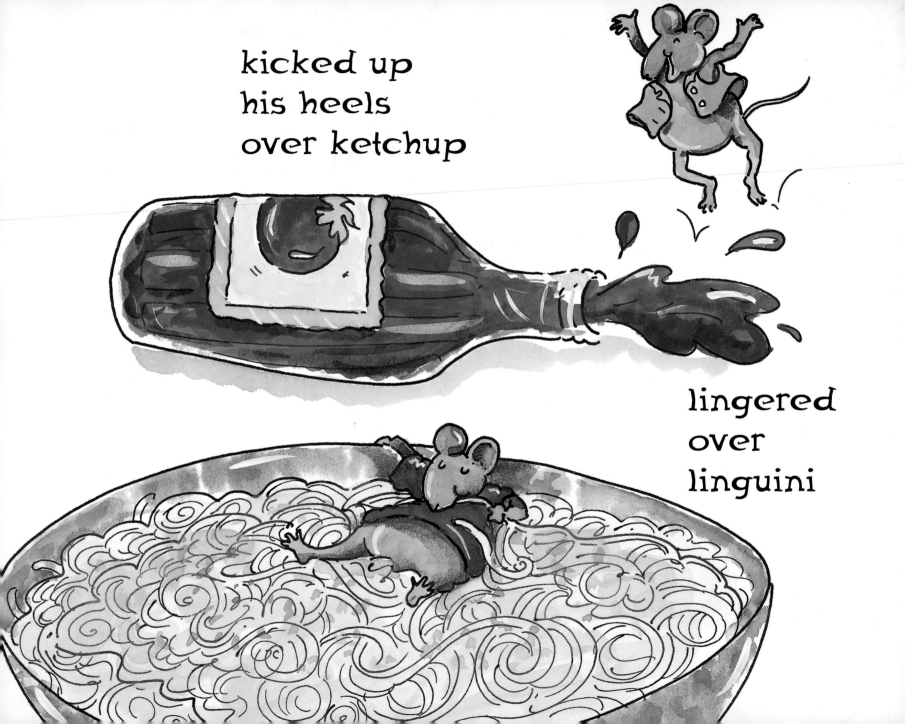

kicked up
his heels
over ketchup

lingered
over
linguini

munched
on
mints

nibbled on nachos

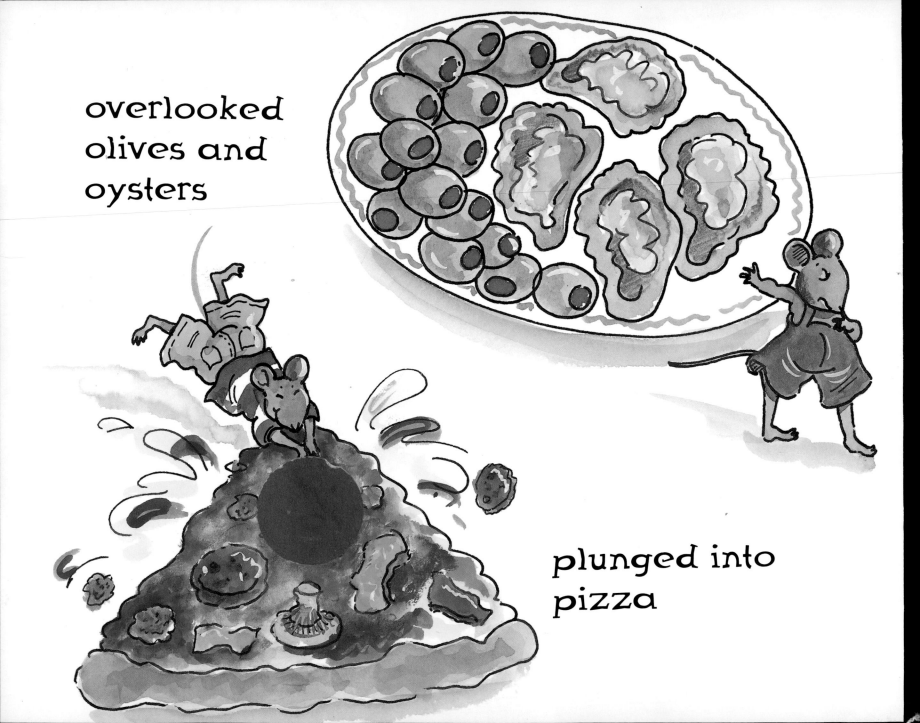

overlooked
olives and
oysters

plunged into
pizza

quietly had quiche

ran after a rolling raspberry

silly over strawberry shortcake

topsy-turvy
for
taffy

unwell after upside-down cake

vigorous from
vegetables

wild over
watermelon

yelled "yummy" for yogurt

zeroed in on zucchini

The friends who ate from a to z,
Were slightly sick and needed tea.